A M E R I S C O P I A

Camino del Sol

A Latina and Latino Literary Series

A M E R I S C O P I A

EDWIN TORRES

The University of
Arizona Press

TUCSON

The University of Arizona Press
© 2014 The Arizona Board of Regents
All rights reserved

www.uapress.arizona.edu

Library of Congress Cataloging-in-Publication Data
Torres, Edwin, 1958–
  [Poems. Selections]
 Ameriscopia / Edwin Torres.
    pages cm. — (Camino del Sol: A Latina and Latino Literary Series)
  ISBN 978-0-8165-3075-5 (pbk. : alk. paper)
  I. Title.
 PS3570.O696A6 2014
 811'.54—dc23
                    2013034408

Publication of this book is made possible in part by the proceeds of a permanent endowment created with the assistance of a Challenge Grant from the National Endowment for the Humanities, a federal agency.

Manufactured in the United States of America on acid-free, archival-quality paper containing a minimum of 30% post-consumer waste and processed chlorine free.

19   18   17   16   15   14   6   5   4   3   2   1

a man once unmanned
            will man what is man
but once he is manned
            a man will unman

me llamo Llame-e-e-e-e-e
            un hombre sin nombre
me llama Llame-e-e-e-e-e
            y ahora soy hombre

i live as a ma-a-a-a-n
            a man of no name
my name is Unma-a-a-a-n
            unman i remain

CONTENTS

IV

AMERISCOPIA

I Wanted to Say Hello to the Salseros but My Hair Was a Mess

We were driven to the airport after performing
the night before, at a Hispanic Festival in Columbus Ohio.
A salsa band from California
and a poet from New York — both Puerto Rican
except for my hair.

I had gone too long between haircuts
undecided, after a life of short hair
whether I had what it takes to look good with long hair.
Did I possess the physicality to balance
my scrawny calves — which magnified
with every pound I imagined . . . if I had long hair?

After years of Tang milkshakes & individually wrapped
american cheese slices, would my non-existent upper-body strength
hold up to what I'd always envisioned?

During this indecision, it grew quickly
into one lump.
        My hair, represented
a non-barrio dryness, unkept — almost
hippie-like, something that just
wouldn't sit too well with the busload
of Boricuas I was riding with.

Here were traditional Puerto Rican Men,
from 20 years of age to 60 — very well groomed
with gold watches and wisecracks.
Here I was, feeling out-of-place as my
very non-Puerto Rican glasses kept slipping . . .
I was having thoughts of fitting in or not.

        If you even have thoughts
of fitting in or not, you don't.

my beard may be trimmed
                but my hair is disheveled
        in my head
                is my entire conundrum

The rear-view mirror exposed a rear view
of who I was supposed to be in this Latino Age.
All because of my hair — adding to my previously
mentioned, generally non-Puerto Rican look.

Thing is, I'm the first to not want to fit in
anywhere! When the moment you're in — stops
to surround you — with memory and cologne
you take what's around you, as immediate past
smiling into the future — flowing into the ebb.

On a bus ride with my brethren
us Latinos — we are gracious in our handouts.
Unconscious demonstrators of our plight, whether real
or imagined. It's convenient to have purpose
if there *is* plight . . .
old Salseros never die, they just find another beat.

        I'm from here they're from there
        we're brought to the middle of the land
        to show what the edges are like

        each coast represents
        an island of coasts
                        obscure
                                revolving around myself
                                        I can see
                each of my coasts
                        staring me back
                                in the rear-view mirror

                an island of who I am
                        unsteady —
                                against the land I'm in

: :

Puerto Rican men are all my father, there's
no getting around that I can't help it — I know
it's not true, but the brain tells me
what the music won't.
                              And the music tells me
now — what my mother used to then, silent
as the morning he died.

All Puerto Rican men
are Salseros with impeccable timing,
just like my father — finally
taking me for a grown-up haircut
the day before he died.
                              Little ten-year-old mop-top
spending the afternoon with dad, first and only
time — meeting his grown-up friends
at my uncle's store — I need to use
the bathroom, I said.
                              He winked at the men
and told me where it was.

I turned on the light — all four walls
the ceiling and parts of the floor
were covered with pictures of naked women.
There wasn't an empty space
anywhere . . . centerfolds, playmates, legs
and hips and who knows what — a sea of flesh
and glossy eyes watching me pee.

I finished quick, and came back to my father.
He said, How was it. I said, Fine. They all laughed.
As we left for my haircut he gave me a wink.
Letting his guard down for a second,
just like —

all Puerto Rican men, and I used to believe
I wasn't one because I was in touch
with my feminine side — each of my hemispheres
fully occupied — unlike
the uneven beauty of my father.

I discovered that, this world uncovered
is like the soul
of The Puerto Rican man — occupied
by the weight of his balance   between
                                        I
                              and
                                land
… but my vision blurs as my glasses slip.

I'm in regression — against any liberation
that's happened to the species
since the day he died.
                    I refuse progress
because then — everyone will have caught up to me …
and where will I be!

I'm here
as a Puerto Rican Man of New York Soul …
representing my people
by being who I am, confused
and alienated by my own soil — which has now
become my hair.

Sutra

I want you to know
that collected here
is a *gathered* action
over the *form* of action

that is, allowing
the idea of *here*
to be in many chambers
looking for some

to close, others
to fill, let me just
get this out
before I wake and realize

I'm just a plaything
for judgement
a collection of entrances
arranged

by impossible history
a drop
skimmed lightly
under a raindrop's

cover
that is, what *here*
was
unattached by *here*

Waiting Outside the Cafe

I'm waiting at the door of infamy
outside the Poets Cafe, waiting past an hour
for the roots of a movement
to show up, on a sunny day in the lower E.

I see Second Street across Third Street
past the project wall-ways — the Lord is a reverb
bouncing in the alley . . .
>   *rail my sorrow tongue-talk deep, yehhh . . .*
>   *raise your voice my sin-pulled sheep, yehhh . . .*
. . . or was that *your* sorrow? *my* voice?
Inner crossroads confirm, that I am six-deep
in the eyes of the Lord.

My call to respond is recorder, I am Memorex to the live.
To the living I am microphone of humanity, picking up
every firey head, every 2 PM drug addict.
Recorder of praised defeat & damaged darling,
I am painsong for sorcerers, I see *whyknows*
& *whoreover some*, at the feet of change . . .
I continue to wait.

>   . . . mind wanders . . . s'gonna happen any minute now — know how
>   you wait for something in mind — and until that mind
>   comes to something you let yours wander 'cause otherwise
>   you waste all this good wandering your mind wants to do . . . ?
>   Nothing worse than a good wander wants to waste itself — be
>   yours — be yer'own — newly uncovered rat
>   now 15 years later — same rat.

Eons ago, I walked in similar daytime,
before Cafe, before words, high on my twenty-something stench.
Memory shifting into non-employed mode, sunny aftermath
of long night sex-less.
Broken down door, midst of wasteland

suburbia, AlphaBlue City.
Pack dam shadow, cries from a Swedish Loca, sunny hangover
from a French kiss.
Teeth pry teeth apart — early morning glimpse
of poems yet to be, sloshing in saliva yet to find a home.

Tough tongueing for a lashing, years ago . . .
gouging a goner
a gash — for licking long legs gone wrong.
Mocha Night memory, slow and dumb — I caught on later,
adult.

      The Later Adult —
      comes into own lateness, a
      dolt!
      A matre of dots!
      A pull-ter of malt!
      Hateness!
      Mate-Flag!
      I am flying my Mate Flag
      Waving . . . "Why"
            "Y"
            "Why You Late . . . Señor'rican?"
Neuro-ligueno?
Neurological Rican?
Neu-Rico-Lenguo . . . amma
Lingo-Rican witta disorder — offa, duh tongue!

      When you're talking about everything
      to someone who isn't there . . . it's like, everything's in front of you
      and you've disappeared.

I had everyone in my apartment, we all
stared at each other, music of metal inching up my leg.
I was cool one with apartment of pink
and cool blue was the window we all stared at.
Each reflection was us — we was the glass we was, you know —
they all had slicked acid
and me . . . I was goon.

Invited host at my own tomb.
Never had drugs, this was all
in my room . . . conversation turned to Chinese light, flicker of it all.
I was designated rider, watching the rise from across the hall.

How young we were in our tired little bodies.
How ahead everything was when no one was there.

Who's more Latin than Latino I?
Dropping off vowels witta mis-placed sigh!

There is excitement to the exotic fruit.
The spice of the uncontrollable is irresistible to the taste bud, suffering
misery of same dinner, over and over. Be spicy and hurt me
so I can remember you. Be the shiver in the earthquake's mainline
fixing a straddle between two rides —
two rips gouged out of sky. Be the boy
who gets to be the man, by the end of the sentence — in the same poem
even. Be the promise forming on the haze
of a Nuyorican morning — colliding
with whatever's waiting
outside this door.

Apartment 5D

morning drops, outside my door, a new day delivered, for all to hear, in a city apartment
with *no* dog, running in *no* front yard, chasing *no* paperboy, a hallway, between *we*
and *world*, a door, separating *us* from *morning*, arriving, with orange skyshift to
cloudless grey, as day wants

to think, how *screwy* ocean heart, how *mellow you* to choose *tasty me*, before the
drop, the *jolt* of orange sky, *shift* to cloudless dew, or *blue* as day would
say, how *echo* of you to *repeat* my glow, to *word* on what we heard *just then*, how
gloriousness we, how *lightful* sent this peeking love, between *we*

and *world*, *no* fence, *no* grass, how *where* to go, what swallows the massive tooth,
the running whip of machine, what follows *form* behind *terror*, *time*—*to go* you
say, *so soon?* waves—dirt—mud—crest—noise—*ravage* the body system, the silent
chamber locked by load, the entirety of embellishment, full—city—noise

a *next* stilled for a few days, an amount of hours *built* without sound, *isolated* from
its shell, *removed* of obstruction, a *crag* cutoff by smackfest jab, the harbor cove's
undisciplined rejoinder crammed upswing the foot, where fever *flivers on* the
moment you step out of that comfort shrill, all that *morning jazz* attached to you

your innocent ears, *a sponge*—the walk of your everyday, *a push*—who was just now
Shakespeare in a Bird cage, who paid me a visit, my kingdom come, I walk up your
hill, up the village gold, the braiding pond from Harlem, who was *just now* waving
Echo and Paris, who gave me fingers to *flop* on words

immersion fluid seeks fowl, who takes a breath, *take one*—and let *knock me* visit,
a shanty-rant up *sense*—here, I'm so tired, *I'd sleep to dream up more words for you . . .*
dear neighbor, but I'd only have to wake up again—*vitamin me* slips a notch below
reason, how I stayed avoiding the *out*, when I stepped out *the out* stepped in

oh gloriousness sound machine
oh invigourous explanatious
oh sonora del contusida
oh countess morn
oh failing give
oh tight reminder
lightly spent envisioner
gastric denumerator
oh late newspaper of day of hour
oh man . . . where to go with this

Temporality at 5 AM

Catching every moment, so I have it
Because what if I lose every bit of my time
Every thought, in a word, a letter
here on the page in front of me

The receptacle *being* managed
By the *output*
What is mine, to lose
Would be shared, to win

Who am I to say what is victorious
A family that sleeps on one bed, the size of a floor
Underneath a ceiling fan in the dark
A twilight, appearing to a sleepless eye, as corona

Melted blue by starlit blade
Moon in chimes of five made two
Because of catching, throwing made itself *second*
Leaving *falling* as orphan

What if I fall
In every moment I fail to catch
Because I get up
Instead of fall back

To catch this moment, on this page
What if I lose this moment
To all the others I've caught
All the others

Waiting their turn
To be read, breathed into
Re-lived as new, how many new ones
Does anyone really need

Exhausting
To get up and write this down
Again, to catch the light
As it dawns

To go back and fall again
To meet pillow looking up
To say *what* again, you know…
To stare at a ceiling you can't see

The Circle at One End

a street knows *dark*
intimate   with night
every turn — clicked
on neon's reassembled *no one*

— an empty man
— an older memory
would that play
as   reminder or warning

no clear answer
is the answer   — would that be
foreplay   or determination
(if vultures
could only *deep* —

how to complete what physics say
is
unphysical — space, time
or light

what circle
to side with   when the opening
is in constant shift — *me* and *her*
in process
(because there is always
a *her* —

stiletto *us* — give each other
timeless mobility
in our fractals   our glorious
fractals — we *lift*

with light   and *quake*
in shades of mutation
but — when does
wonder into our *want*
(want
our *me* or *her* —

here   is my *move*
what I believe in
what I want to pass on
to *you* — here

is my *filter*
what I use for noise —
my *infiltration masquerade*
my *makeup* — here is the gloss
I cover my *stains* with
(my *alphabet*   invented
my cryptic *magnification* —
          my *embarrassment*
my human potential
for *things* — much larger
than what I see

my *face*   a fulcrum
of recognition, my *fast*
my *faster*, my tessellate *faculty*
disguised   as pride
(my handsome *walk*
in the fires of *talk* —

          isolation — my sometime *sunshine*
my *platform*
entrenched — in the ashes
I stand on

here is my *point*
my *shaved* encounter   with something
larger than what I catch —
something so large

so open, so necessarily
broken
that I kept it, held it, trusted
that *you* — would want it
(unrequited, unadorned   here
at the end —

The Necessariest
(a discussion with duchamp & tanguy)

> the most necessary nearest
> is not at most pl*ced by self
>
> the alln*ss of pl*ce
> as necessary nesting
>
> the antagonist pugilist
> absent of pounding, *l*m*nt (*as such*)
>
> lacking most expression is . . .
> what's missing
>
> a sense of hum*r
> pieces of scr*p . . . really
>
> an action
> transcending pl*ce
>
> pliant expl**n*d in a moment, but . . .
> I d*n't kn*w
>
> *
>
>> river a word (*rather abruptly*)
>
> in a time of anxiety, rising røos, in a time of relieved
> quality, a willing of acceptance, of don't have a quality,
> of a time that dies, out of irony, a time when the public
> will get mad
>
> in a something great, a time of improvement, my friend,
> interesting young and machine-like, is machine, built of machine,
> art machine of the garden, somehow dedicated to machine,
> friend to friend of himself, imagined by his own friendship,
> to whom is machine but machine-him
>

> homage to destruction, a destroyed place, highly
> chance-like, a great one thing, the machine in flames, that
> didn't center off it, the machine of himself, uncentered
> somewhere, for them, the originators of machine, what would
> hardly destroy a series of giants, waiting
>
> a choir waiting, a young tingle waiting, a shiver, a ripple
> unskinned, waiting, waiting, a finger, an army, waiting to pull
> itself, holding a misunderstanding, a capital, a sheet of
> paper, a self, a borrowed ahem, a clearing of the ahem, a
> castle, throat art, there was a machine that destroyed this
> young friend of mine, this man, artistic man, these men,
> willing and cleared, by pl*ce
>
> a great anxiety, ten developed into two, a sui fenned by
> space, alphatogs developed into numerals, popped by
> speaker, eternalent pointillistic firmament, writ by muse,
> how inspiring the unspeaker, this unheard of country,
> this all american, fired upon, what I was hearing,
> feedback to men, as human as one can be, without gender
>
> fine indiffident flatness, not only the public, was the
> pervert, but into the interest was the seeing, not only
> entertainment but real fight, pugilismo, the idea behind the
> fight, no antagonist, no protest, all they did, all these
> men did, all my friend destroyed, pull the plug, they had
> to, what, otherwise, completely rosed, d'ya see that, to who,
> to what was lacking the elemental, a good antagonism, a
> machine work, a friend without gender, a nothing that was
>
> nothing without the public, who talks like they know it,
> who initiates change, who is objectified by acceptance, but
> what is here is, everything accepted, mentality of junk, of
> space, of Jung, of agreement, who is public but who stays
> home, time to sign anything, a mass of anger, what would
> angrify the audience, an intense no, a more, of our
> existential, of want, of who I want, you angry? . . . give me
> a chance to pull one over, to sometimes disappear, to live
> in things that are true
>

> a kind of incredible intelligence, wills into emphasis,
> cares about, who is public and who is human, is the part, of
> you that destroys, is the ride a beginning, a society, or only
> part of, we, into our games, obligations of conviction,
> aesthetic language, by any two, any one

Father Song

open the stubborn wound
impossible division

driven by dusk
wind's palpitation

minor son
trowel escape

with hereness
pasted onto

slivered disc, this
the momentary sibling

to nightly destina
cracked, to core

wayward dawn
monstrous brayer

stripped, across my level
I was just now seeing you

before my opening crayon
and I was thinking

you with your butterfly wings
and yoga thumbs

before you fell off your icy road
33 years ago

did you have me in your head
as your only son

or as the son you never had

Fixative

My mom is a picture of health. Every inch a child where I used to be. We have a turtle that lives in the fridge. In the vegetable tray. In the bottom. Sometimes we feed it cabbage but mostly its life is there in the empty tray. A hard shell. A bald head. One day I come home and see that mom has cleaned my luggage like she said she would. I'd been away on a short trip. My 18-piece luggage made of thick wash-basin porcelain had accumulated dust. It is extremely heavy and awkward to maneuver, its bulk outweighing its purpose. But it protects unusual items that need protection. Upon my return, my mother saw the dust and the frustration on my face. She said, "I'll fix it." I came home. Each porcelain piece had been wallpapered with fake wood grain so that it would appear lighter. "Mom, how did you do that?" I marveled. "It's only luggage," she answered. My mom saw that I was hungry and said, "I'll fix it." I went to wash my face, came into the kitchen and there was mom, serving me green soup in the huge turtle shell. "Mom, why did you do that?" I asked. "It's only a turtle," she said. I had to leave for the airport and was running late. My mother saw that I was worried and said, "I'll fix it." She pulled the car to the front, my luggage strapped to the roof. "Get in," she said. The radio playing, past the speed limit, a Brazilian song comes on with my mother's voice, singing the chorus in Spanish, I was astonished. "Mom, when did you record this?" "It's only music," she said. On the airplane my mother calls me on my cellphone. "Did you get to the airport?" she asks. "Yes, you dropped me off," I remind her. I keep her on the line and return to the crossword puzzle waiting on my seat. I ask her if she knows of a six-letter word for fixative. She hangs up. The stewardess notices my perplexed face and places an envelope with the word "now" on my lap. I open it. Inside is a note from my mother. I think to myself, how did she do that? I read the note. It says, "It's only a puzzle."

~~~

The stewardess notices my perplexed face and places an ice box on my lap. The word "now" etched in frost on the outside. I open it and there's a note from my mother inside. I think to myself, mom how did you do that? I read the note. It says, "It's only a puzzle."

~~~

The stewardess notices my perplexed face and places an ice box on my lap. I open it. Inside is an envelope, and a baby turtle eating cabbage. I open the envelope and eat the note. I think to myself, how did I do that?

~~~

The stewardess notices my perplexed face and places a baby turtle on my lap. I look at her and she walks away. I think to myself, mom?

~~~

The stewardess notices my perplexed face and removes her gloves. Her face comes close to mine as she leans in. She strokes the left side of my face and whispers, "mom."

~~~

The stewardess notices my perplexed face and removes her gloves. Her face comes close to mine as she leans in. She strokes the left side of my face with her left hand. She places her right hand on my lap and unzips my suitcase. She gently prys my teeth apart with her tongue and pulls my turtle out of its shell. And I think, mom?

~~~

The stewardess notices my mom.

~~~

The mom.

Moth

I'm walking in the morning sunlight, the sidewalk attracts a moth. It looks like it's wounded since it remains in one spot, fluttering around this one spot. As if it's either getting sun or else eating a sidewalk bug, I can't tell. I'm curious and worried for it. I stop walking. I bend my head down, not the entire body. The body remains rigid, hat on straight, looking down as if I were a lighttower whose beam had focused down. A man is walking towards me. Yellow top. Dark skin. Taller than me. He comes closer. The sun streaming through open leaves. Dappled shade follows his long limbs. Patterns of morning looking. I'm sure he'll wonder what's made me stop and bend my neck like this. I'll point out the moth I say to myself. Excited with the possibility of shared discovery. Look at this, I say as he comes towards me. He doesn't break stride, steps on the moth, and keeps moving. I keep walking. Further down the path I'm in the open sun where the leaves have stopped. I see another moth fluttering on the sidewalk. And then two more. As if getting morning sunbaths or eating special sidewalk bugs, I still can't tell. I remain rigid, aware of my height as I tower over them. I cross the road where the sun is brightest and there's hundreds of them. All fluttering low on the sidewalk. Not nature. A grey and brown pattern of wings in flight, staying still. A texture of moving ground. As if the concrete were trying to stand up after a lifetime of lying down. Erupting in waves of failed attempts.

Water

I am the guest of a prince. I stay at his palace and share my room with two other talents. The three of us are unique and in demand. We are each 10 stories tall. We do what we do and what no one else does. Our limbs are a hike, folding path over glory. I wake up one morning and look out the window. An ocean has appeared. Its surface, 10 stories above me, the sun just arriving. A reef reaching towards me through clear blue water crystalized by morning's shimmer. A surface broken by shadows, underneath what appear to be cliffs. The ocean bottom, as deep as I am from the surface, 10 stories below. I am 10 stories above. 10 is where we meet. I look down. A horse is swimming into view. Its mane whipped by morning windwater. The horse is alone for an instant. Free for a few kicks. Then a rider appears on its back. Instantly not free. The rider is a tourist on an underwater swimming tour, where the horse does all the swimming. I turn my head and see more enter the frame. 10 more. 10 signifying more than height, horse, or story. Against the blue-green water, the ocean bottom is visible. Horse and rider float. 10 stories above me. In slow motion, sounds like. But that's because storyteller remains in the story. They swim away. The water clears as if almost to disappear. My eyes adjust and see 10 surfer punks relaxing at the bottom of the ocean. They wear cut-off jeans and shorts. Some have t-shirts some don't. They are relaxing in chaise lounges on the bottom of the floor, getting sun tans through the crystal clear water. Every few seconds, one of them swims up to the surface for a gulp of air and swims back down. The scene is a constant yo-yoing of bodies going up and down. Swimming with hands to sides, long hair flowing behind, air bubbles tracing their destination. Up and down. Up and down. A hypnosis of breath and water. A reward at bottom and at top. A kind of water that lets this happen. A kind of animal doing what nothing else can.

II

Father to Father

it has been too long
since I've seen my father's grave
I can remember the grass,
its shape, the weeds spelling out
how long it's been

I can smell the flowers
left by my aunt
reminding me how she visits
with a frequency
any brother would cherish

the row of tombstones
the cars passing by
the umbrellas when I was little
the cake and coffee at
grandma's house afterwards

I can sense the desperation
as I walk between the rows
on top of graves
searching for where I thought he was
once again

am I trying to live through you
imagining you as I could never be
is this what I need to resolve
before becoming a father
before the legacy you've left me takes root

let's have a talk pop
when you left
I barely had a grip on what you were
what I'd become
and I'm still that boy imagining himself a man

but what is that supposed to be
pops, what does it mean to say *man*?
is your legacy pride disguised
as machismo, the conflict
of the new age puerto rican

why don't you let me find you
there are beautiful people
who find themselves trapped
and no matter how often
they are told how beautiful they are

never believe it
until one day it happens
and that self-worth
is what completes them
and I don't know

if it's you or me that needs to be told
but one of us is beautiful
so just let me find you
I've met men who have shown me
heard their conversations

seen apparitions, witnessed the actions
of what would form a father figure
put all that together in my head
and still I find myself
tripping over something that used to be there

let me find you
maybe you're hiding
maybe you do need to be told
maybe what it comes down to
is you and me

talking man to man
whatever that means to you

A Minotaur Sleeps on Shelter Island

This is the tale of Minotaur
and his best friend Helio-lite
who was a tiny yellow bird always on his shoulder
guiding Minotaur through his labyrinth

After a lifetime of slaying,
Minotaur expired
he left his creatures, his mountains, his rivers, everything
to little Helio-lite

Helio-lite said goodbye
to Minotaur
and promised he would continue
Minotaur's legacy

Minotaur smiled
from his massive Minotaur mouth,
flitted his ears, and slept
for years—Helio-lite

Kept his promise
flying in and out
of the labyrinth, his tiny wings
carrying his golden body

He was much tinier
than Minotaur
but had learned secrets
that made him just as feared

Over time—the chore
of slaying lost souls
and maintaining all this land
grew to be too much

Little Helio-lite needed a rest
a long rest—so, out of respect,
he went to Minotaur's grave
and asked for his blessing

He then returned to the labyrinth
and closed it—forever,
instead he planted seeds
gathered from all his land

Flowers and trees
from around the kingdom
were now growing where prisoners
had lost their way

What once was fearful
was now a garden
with statues in three pieces
and sunshine splintered in petals

Satisfied—little Helio-lite
left the garden and went
to the mountains to live out
the rest of his tiny days

One morning Helio-lite
woke to the sun—chirping
his golden-yellow song as usual, but this time
the sun was a mirage

Helio-lite looked around the sky—
the mountain itself
was a mirage—Helio-lite was confused
and searched for his favorite tree

There it is!—he flew excited
and ran smack into its mirage
with a force so hard it knocked him backwards
and put him right to sleep

The next morning Helio-lite woke up—
on Minotaur's shoulder
hello nice to see you!—said Minotaur
Helio-lite realized what happened

And was happy to be back
with Minotaur—hello
nice to see you too! and Minotaur
took him to their labyrinth garden

Where flowers were free
and trees were wild
and the only thing trapped
was forever

E.G. as I.E.

Crescent sliver slips unseen
Talks me through dusk
And the unobserved worship that happens
Between *glance* and *answer*

Which one is maker
Of what everyone sees
From *darkspot* to *remove*
Melt *planet* from *plane*

Dear venus —(*for example*)
Tell me about reticulation
And the microscopic rip between
Finger and *myth*

A treasured extinction, to be *same*
And *as* in mid-flight
Pasted up there
Star canvas iridescent

And me down here
Between chains
Immediate, pointed, turning
Locked inside a listen

Open millennium
Waves me through
Convinces vanity
Of connectivity —(*in explanation*)

What can't be taken
Willfully ruins *how*
Before *why* shows up —threadbare
As a dialogue assumed

One Wave Walking to Four Phases of the Moon

If first day of any first—is phase
What to make of Sun—when new
   With time—when is new to time
Who only lives—in new

Moon tells walk—to re-chance
Talk to invent—late
   Alive—with late
Interior will follow invention—as new sun

On all fours—will follow moon
To talk bumps—to inherit the coming glow
   Each out—reshaped to surround
Again each haze—to brace

    At every landing—how quick
To lose interest—without the bruise

Neptune's Elegia

he wanted to face what he did by taking a walk on the sand with his words and papers behind him in the trail of his shadow the sun waited to surprise him with the start of what would soon become his story in the time of his breath a second sun appeared as an ear for what would soon become his mouth a momentary breeze enlivened his step and tried to become a body between both suns shielding his eyes he covered his walk from the storm by grabbing his papers as they swirled around him each shadow attempted to catch each step as his words were now etched against a wall of wind and sand each sun remained on one side each eye on the other as he saw what he'd become by reaching through the mouth of the one ahead of him dropping sand from his fingers while caught in his storm each start emerged as a reminder of story what kept him in story   what burned in his walk

The Vase of the Universe

Gull shanty red rot
Flecting the slay, the kill-off, the pounding . . .
Angry as anger.
Catalysting its severed lick over the scrubbed grain
Of razerboard abracadabras.

White wisurled heightened amandas . . . again and again,
Over salapocketed grandeur. Battering
The sainted grains of mint-shining lifers.
Corpuscled shiv-splinted, innerly dormant
By sin-pinted blood twicer.

Water beast white pieces of the vase of the universe.
Broken and scattered
A quirl, a core, a few of which landed on
This pounding shore.
Pounding and angry as anger, for my feet to discover,
Where the skin of its shell
Gathers harmonies of color from similes of skies.

Alabaster jubilees dancing in the shards.
A translucent drip.
A cone quirling a shallow hurl.
A shimmer on the face.
A stone.
Shoots waves of bloated gods through surrender's chanteuse.

Ocean spray kilter, gulls' shanty red rot.
Battered beacher preach prancer
Beat-listen to sing-memories, yellow bead stilter . . .
Slay to the kill-off
Bead rat-shatted milkness, a lactating temptress on fire-wet shatters.

Scorns of slings in my slip
Pound my palling palkadine surf.
Shoes grounded yellow-grey to gravity (fulled falstaff dismembrance)
Fools her earth spiral sand, musing her sheet-sanded swoon.

White wither rotting amandas,
Again and again . . . angry as anger
Sound suncanting canter round, pounding
Pieces of shayered-frieze.
Seized tier,
By tier,
By hues . . . falled from vase.

Scattered this to shore, kiss
To my foot sanded hoot.
Slay to the kill-off, the keel-bow
Bevacqua-fleece hunter, Fishwisher-Galopia,
Glowing with tidal rememory.

My salient galaxies knife these cuticles of phosphoressence.

In magining-gentle-agenta-kin plumage . . .
In puddling-quellemine-green-fluttered swear . . .
Sworn to tide eternal vase, there. Holding swigs
Of salapockets, bare, nary bigguns . . . rip-ride
Bated saint, gladiator of fin paramours.

Bake a tail for an x or a fool . . . or
Flirt undilate-skirt undertow taut with glow caught,
By Prophet-Sail, the salt to my sea-line ablutions.
Healing her broken her ceiling the floor, her dust
A blue spiral spoken. Quiet, quirl-vessantly
Shushed to shore, I soar . . .

A sky bows her headwind shyward, while ravailing seaward.
Under the slip, jigs the forgiving membrane . . .
A seaweedled camel, burp
Dunking the hump of the cosmos. Cormorant runner

Shoots a dot-pitted sun, combing the run
Of this pounding . . . again and again.

A redbill dubby.
A webber.
An eye starin' stub.

A chick barely
Cheeked
With shy-shiny crubs.
      Craw, Craw, the hoot will fly . . .
      High, High, the krill goes nigh . . .
Sainted lifer, hold waters of blood
And spill blooded twicer.

On the shores of above, sunning a drowsy z . . .

Ellabyrinth

Elaborate
Ellabyrinth blinded
Breakening my allusions to
Creationing

Phome
Phomic tomes my
Illusions to awakening—a scraped reed
Along a moon
Chanting

Tonic scales
Seventh everenth hue
Second un in many ways
Encoiled
Impaled in Raga

Pointed
Palms
Elaborythine—your throat of granite
Premonize mine—voice canyon
Rising
Stringing
Octaves of shine
Gyrations of melancholy
Resonate with illusion, whales and elephants
Of red and clay

You live in shadows
I live in light
Both of us—engorged in saga

Tiny reedless gander
You are my thoughtless look
Louder than the sun
Whose instrument is a labyrinth
Of tones entombed

Air Is Sham for Light

I am air
and I know air — as
air I am
          I
          walk cloud mounts
          -tains, hunds an' thous's
                    at the ridge of my glowho, I *so* passé
                    see so low I *most* air
                    when I plow through I
see sun as hole
through I go, sun is through "I
defeat you" says I
          in story I
          in hole
          grab hold of toe, go south
                    a flash of light 't' ning
                    and I, so rare
                    am steady beath' a leu above vanue

c'est suis je-je-jet-mon avenu des cleurs, des-onnes
ó dos o bechy rebee bo co si no,
o si so yo, so nosi noise-si . . . was a so, was I so noisy, was a

          so, it was — I
          red eyes
          of grand sa-
                    tan, great land
                    I call forgery, no-was-me was my
                    constitute, a bully to the rest - o' - tute
                              everywhere I go
                              I am payed to stay over the naked trees
                              dressed of air — now in smoke I saw
the eyes that pulled me through
in smoke and now I ground
in grey sound I

and now I stay
am I
on ground
     am air on ground
     I only see . . .
     what wants to overtake me — air
          as coagulated mass
          consumes — air
          as fog around denial, what I don't want to say, what
     prevents me from admission
     of this vile life *but*
     I
who drown the sun in time
who wrap her ray 'round mine, who
but I
as *strangeled* as I
was I — air?
was I — truth? as fog that
          forms
          from hole
               floating over mouth, smoke
               screen overtakes
               me my body, I
am light — no, I am
          radiance, vomit of light
leftover disaster once light is done
          I am scattered inchoate disaster, jazzimony trip-
               lication, imagi-mo-tion passive
     a-passion regressive
          temptant, devilish dashante
             a sham — for sunshine

Song of the Red Lamb

Who Lives On That Lamb Red -
Who Lives On That Lamb Red -
Who Lives On That Lamb Red - - Leg
Who Lives On That Lamb Red - - Leg
(Please Help Me Out)   - That Lamb Red
Who Lives On That

              (eg)(head) -   ministration
In This - -   recessional
In That - -   infra-sssss-tration
In This - - mensingal-tense-in-sin-t-uation

Who Lives On That Lamb Red -
Who Lives On That Lamb Red -
(Who Lives On That)
          Please Help -
(Who Lives On That)
          Please Help - Mmmmbbbb
            Help Me By - increntation
            Help Me By - incrimination
            Help Me By - incronstraintion
            Help Me By - incretination
                    - insinuation
                    - concentration
                    - ensentation
                    - infenestration
                    - penestration
                    - mecegenation
                    - mommentration
                    - penancesation
                    - flagemation
                    - magination - - This

Uni Masta-mmmmmmmation' - mmmm
More lies on That - fffffrusss - tration
Moola issa - penetration - fulla - fenestration
              (Please Help Mmmmbbbb)
              (Please Help Mmmmbbbb)
              (Please Help Mmmmbbbb)
Who Lives On That Lamb Red -
Who Lives On That -

Viva La Viva

I used to be the picture of a family man
I used to have insurance and a family plan
I used to be a fixture for the family man
I used to have endurance for the family plan
viva la lala, lala, la lalalala
viva la lala, lala, la lalalala
viva la lala, lala, la lalalala
viva la lala, lala, la lalalala
I used to have a garden with a place in the sun
I used to have a shoulder I could lay my head on
I used to be the model of a bodily soul
I used to hide a bottle in the watering hole
viva la lala, lala, la lalalala
viva la lala, lala, la lalalala
viva la lala, lala, la lalalala
viva la lala, lala, la lalalala
I used to be the leader of a nation of woe
I used to push a button and the missile would go
I used to blow the whistle on the fizzle below
I used to put the sugar in the cappuccino
my people suffer more than yours do
my people suffer more than yours do
my people suffer more than yours do
my people suffer more than yours do
viva la lala, lala, la lalalala
viva la lala, lala, la lalalala
viva la lala, lala, la lalalala
viva la lala, lala, la lalalala
I used to have a limo but they took it away
I used to have a pillow but they took it away
I used to have a baby but they took it away
I used to have a maybe but they took it away
I used to watch the enemy before it was me
I used to watch the battle be the battle I see
I used to watch theology be all you can be
I used to watch reality before a tv

when people suffer they go d-d-d-dumb
when people suffer they go d-d-d-dumb
when people suffer they go d-d-d-dumb
when people suffer they go d-d-d-dumb
I used to beat around the bush and call it a day
I used to peter out about a third of the way
I used to pay attention to the mention of new
I used to have a useta be addiction to you
viva la lala, lala, la lalalala
viva la lala, lala, la lalalala
viva la lala, lala, la lalalala
viva la lala, lala, la lalalala
I used to be the color of the people I know
I used to be the lover of the people I know
I used to be the brother of the people I know
I used to be the other of the people I know
I bet a better booty's gonna better the flow
I beat a better booty witta bubble o'blow
I better let a booty be the buddha below
a buddha better beat it if he doesn't belong
I used to suffer but I d-d-d-don't
I used to suffer but I d-d-d-don't
I used to suffer but I d-d-d-don't
I used to suffer but I d-d-d-don't
you ever get a feeling life is passing you by
you ever get a feeling you could never describe
you ever get a feeling you were never alive
you ever get a feeling I could take you alive
I used to be much thinner when a thinner was fun
I used to be the sinner when a sinner was fun
I used to be the winner when a winner was fun
I used to have fun now I'm holding a gun
some people suffer and go p-p-p-pow
some people suffer and go p-p-p-pow
some people suffer and go p-p-p-pow
some people suffer and go p-p-p-pow
viva la lala, lala, la lalalala
viva la lala, lala, la lalalala
viva la lala, lala, la lalalala
viva la lala, lala, la lalalala

Ode

this is a poem to the rhythm of life
this is a poem to the rhythm of life
this is the rhythm of a minimal life
this is the rhythm of a minimal life

I'm tryin' to settle to the rhythm of life
but all along I'm on a minimal high
I set a level to the rhythm of life
but every minute is a minimal life

I wrote a poem to the rhythm of life
I found the words upon a liminal sky
when I was young it was so easy to lie
but is a man who says it better than I

some ever said it was a sever society
so ever civil is it ever the piety
my scissor pacifism is a reality
but seminism is a seminal masterpiece

don't ever let me get ahead of my lie
don't ever say I never told you the right
don't ever bet on a believable lie
don't ever say it was a minimal life

this is the rhythm of a minimal life
this is a poem to the minimal life
this is the rhythm of a minimal life
this is a poem to the rhythm of life

This Is Not the Conversation That I
Started the Conversation With

we're not part of the mainstream
we ARE the mainstream
son, baby, kid ... listen I don't care what you call me
just do it on your own dime
and that's the joke
so I was told, son, baby, kid, see

miguel has this thing about the mainstream
but I ain't seen him for years, son
so does that make *his* stream
the *main* still
or has the *stream* caught up with what it was
he was when *I* was
with him, son, baby, kid, *mijo*, whatever the hero in your lingo be
but

we would have our
one yearly conversation in his car
driving *back* and *to* his class in Rutgers
and there's a cassette tape I have
from one of our trips
where he's talking a blue streak not
cursing blue just
talking *fast* so that makes it *sky*
blue instead of *jet*
but

he got all worked up about
our place in the fabric
of america *our* meaning *us* although
he had a way of flipping what was *said*, with what was *real*
and what *became* real, and turning *me* on, *with* it, or *it*, on *me*, so this
grand exercise in politico
bravura was really extravagant *pointing* of the *self*

telling me to learn about what it was
I was doing in *my* time for
my people cloaked in the fumes
of the jersey turnpike and
machiavellian promise
but

as confused as I was
by such grandeloquent machinations
I was grateful to be included
in the collective *we* of this here *his* statement
since there was *definite* mutual respect showed
regardless of what was
in *these* confined quarters on *his* front seat
on *this* stretch of america's highway, *his*
overtly sexual prowess
brandished fearlessly as one might
a new playing card or in a higher tax bracket
a new maserati in a garden of naked men
but

going back before the ride
before the mainstream laced its light afternoon drizzle
back during lunch after one too many swigs of revised thunderbird—
we are served by the server, what is *meal*
and what is *king*—his barstool inched
he leans in slow says, *I'm gonna show you something baby*
his journal revealed, *this* he says
is my next book
written page by page like a real book, the word *real*
impaled by weight and prophet, by this point
all talk of fitting in or not, *son*
gave way, *kid*
to short chasers and straight shooters, *okay mijo let's go*
in the car we went feeling no pain
the prospect of rain sprinkled with politics a booming baritone
and a ride home was my cue that it was time
to wake up

I feel gooood now he says
if I was to go right now, the car
reaching 80, *I'd die a happy man,*
la la la la la lala lala laaaaaa, he sings
oblivious to wet pavement or gas pedal *la lala la la la*
I like talking to you, which was a way of saying
I like that you listen to me
without interfering to which I respond
translucently his mantle having been lowered
a while back after the verbal seductions
of many a fellow poet
but

still . . .
here we were
fascinated by the legion of clouds above
casting their magic
over the shooting star we were
heading home
on the jersey turnpike

A Season of Beens

    Y'know
these wings, these
wings I own—been railed against
& burned, been tested
too far
    Y'know
this flight, this
flight been on—been shut down
much many times, been
run aground
but
    Y'know
this heart, this
heart much stood—been stilled
in storm, been strong
to it all
and
    Y'know
this crown, this
sun that sits—been put
for a spell, for a season, right there
been put underneath—
for a reason

I Am Trying to Perfect My Assént

I'd like to sliver A-mer-ica
live in a separate A-mer-ica
one that is more of a-ME-rica
the one that I don't THAT'S America

Entering the USA
Leaving *la isla* behind
Leaving *The Atlantic* behind
      (the Atlantic *culito* . . . if you will)
Limping into America's horizon
      (all these ways are ways of same)

America waiting for us
open arms jowled with expectation
and furry eyebrows, dismantling
her stripmall hairdos

Havana No Seño or
Negila or Negril
Gi'tude — but not me . . .

    BIENVENUDO
        TO THE BICOASTAL LENGUA!

Forked tongue mandala—speech so true
splits the tongue . . .
into bi-coastal lesions
as America tries hard to perfect her ASS-ent . . . her AC-cent!

    (oye Sombra . . . wheng deed my Other bekom djur Other?)

    Tongue-iva
    Lady Saliva
    Mounted Imbiber
    Ridin the rider

                    but no one rides wit me
                              'cuz I'm wit me
                         and I ain't no one
                                   see, we all wanna piece o' dat *lengua*

Syllables caught on her ear
            screaming echolalia for the *PaPa-patria*
melt down your moetrics *MaMa-mantra*

Lip-piss-sizing on her back legs, America
            rears up and proudly mounts
Rapunzel's locks, casas blancas, ivory tóres, ebonic flóres,
                  edwin porés — open your bordés
                  and call me you — I'm another taino
                        reachando — por tu

O lonely widow of vari-coastal impunity
            safe against your bargain culture, illegally
aliened by the color of grass—how ironic . . .
            to gain freedom . . .
            you must acquire a card . . .
            the color of nature . . .

        O Merdre-Rica
        O Mer Rica
        O Sea of Rich Chica-CACA
        O-WHO-sica
        O-YOU-sica
        OHMMMM-MALAVA
        PALA-BRAVA . . . MU-sica

        O-CooCOOM-bia
        Hum-BOMB-bia
        Afri-SUM-pica
        Come-COME, miha
        O-MA-MA-rica
        O-PA-PA-rica
        O-WHO-WHO-sica
        O-YOU-YOU-sica

        OH . . .   *I wanna mixup A-mer-ica*
                        live in the other A-mer-ica
                        maybe discover a-ME-rica
                        because I'm alone . . . I'm America

Puerto Rican Astronaut

That the *new black*? Hole-insky! (*knock three times*) Just sayin', got it all figured out. Listen … a sushi chef, right? Always a guy, right? FACT! Lookit up, just sayin' ya got yer deep ocean-clan tradition, right? Top o'which (*slap-slap*) hand o'the woman (*pause*) all wrong temperature t'mold fish. FACT! Just sayin'! Okay now, whatabouta-matador … always a man right? FACT! TRADITION, ya got it! Huh? (*pause*) You kiddin'? (*pause*) She any good? (*pause*) That don't count. Plus, yer woman's basic killer instinct, all maternal. *Poor bull, someone's baby, oh diaper*, THE HOOOORNS … he's gotta live every time! The crowd, waitin' for that long, drawn out, painful thrill, *ooooh, ooooh, bloody, bloody* … ZIP! Ya wit me? Okay, now ya got yer white-collar African-American who can't swim or play hockey … 'cuz o'that small bone in his heel. FACT! Lookit up buddy, Jimmy the Greek, Wikipedia, whatever (*knock three times*). So, there's a female sushi chef, a female matador and a black Olympian swimmer hockey player (*slap-slap*). They shack up in a recently foreclosed one-bedroom adobe condo … get this, in the south of Portugal. Huh? (*pause*) Fine, Long Beach, whatever! So listen … no one's having sex, everyone's got an agent … ya wit me? Big Brother meets Ugly Betty meets that pissed-off chef. This is gold baby! (*slap-slap*) Every week like clockwork, they come home, yur right there, key in the lock, rough day at the office, complainin', playin' cards, shovin' undies, goin' on dates, femino-racial what-not and happenstance, right in yer face! A little chunk a'hootchie zen for yoga yuks … just sayin' (*knock three times*)! Now, okay ready … get this! Surroundin' their spread is a curvy wall o'white pasty-faced bricks … hear me out! Like that great wall over there … whattaya got, Asia … help me out! Whatever! But way smaller … and cheaper. Every now and then a piece comes out, so's you can see the other side. Literal crap for all'em Walmart milfs, like breakin' the fourth wall but without the mess. You know, Beaver … with facial hair, ONLY HE NEVER SHAVES! Pot in the hole … he's all *lala lickly*! Anyways, they fix it, have sangria, whatever (*slap-slap*). Decide to get a roommate. Agree on a Puerto Rican astronaut … HAH! Like one more's gonna make a diff … did I say? (*pause*) Make that two plus two, yeah … kickbacks! So get this … one day, they text the fax machine … what? It's been done? Okay, how about this …

Not So Fast Food

or This May Tend To Go On But It Does End

(after john wieners)

Hugh, 35, and her husband Mary of the infant reminder, 42,
The uteriole cholesterates of lush beaches and swimming,
buxom Dr. Octapella (B.M.) and his rewind button
Dr. Bambini (B.D.), sailing for intimate exposure, "multo multo fagotini," infinity's
of hotels and ten thousand sleepy heavens—where you give me
hellos, mapped by flesh, fertility, pumpkin soup, and one couple's massage
aroused by November Twelfth's
two thousand hells.

> "I am
> thinking of death's head
> when I play
> immigrant card"—Cubby Legume (A.D.).

His dentist Dr. Siri Mascara (B.C.), Punta Cana and
Holland America, my husband Mary and his testicular cycle of
nice things and fun secrets, pandemic Dr. Fifi and her teutonic pudenda
Dr. Snugg Natch, narcoptic jock-lick Sissy, bobblehead boob dip Hugh, 35, and yes
spectacular, Kurt and Kate Flock expecting mounds of invasive kootch
from blooded links, mineral baths, happy endings and
Simone DeBeauvois, masseuse informatoire Dr. Lena Horné, always gold always . . .
a day away, Guadalupe Cheese, quelque chose et mon frere Baba Lu
expanding GE153, nano fido, golden vortex
powered by Stuffit, the occupied rower
sitting on ionic breeze, time remaining
2,023,406,814 hours.

> "I feel
> like I'm about to break
> all the time."

Frail Michelle (B.G.) (before grotto), counter cheeseburger,
little piglet on a table top, always
her twin had more drive but she
had the gift, rosemary beads in fallopian sausage, sky-diving tankard,
super-ego and sleep deprivation.

"I could just
eat
you up"—Zona Brutista (N.G.), justificatory Andrews
human afterall—"where'd you meet her …
online," post-gloital hand job.

Cinnamon and her, legs sticky, very very—
to understand the world of Francis
is to approach Assisi as he would have (F.G.) cockatiel tourquet,
pungent Shakira, Mewarinex Isla Ojo and her rubber pillow Dr. Sleepy.

      "Suck
      it in"—he barked
      as he glared, at her
      tummy   control the ship, by controlling the I.

Mary's erective spectacle, ergo his shorts, tranquil Bahamanian,
surfing and oral hygiene
may be too much to handle, at 42, all his swimmers,
holy water—here … is where you may choose a wink, by wishing away
filth, fertility cruise camel toe, upsize my fries.

      "Who—to me, would be
      you, or Hugh, or
      one could say
      I"—Cameo Stardust.

Sat. & Sun., TV on the radio,
Camino Cyberduck (B.C.), Dr. Katie's gardener, Mr. Flash and his daughters,
"Let me guess, comfort conch—it is
in there"—Mrs. Leathery Bravado and his remote brassiere Dr. Video,
PR handyman Hyno Hymn, a finger gone too far, Omni Giraffe
and Combo #1, El Shango Dificil que dige nada, Silver Digit up the bum, "don't,
say don't, again," birds and bees, skipped dinners and cuddles, an oyster
on a pad of heart-shaped razors, the immaculate trunk of
hibiscus fluffers, a sail around the elegant noodle.

this
may tend
to go on, but it does
end

SPE
CTA
CLE   tries to fall apart—on purpose.

    "I am
    sucking it,
    in"—she whimpered, "Suck it in,
    more"—he commanded.

Conception passenger, romantic fathead, my husband Mary and his
eighteen hundred dollar sex expert Dr. Lana Holstein,
her husband Dr. Betty Duff, the chapel of St. Agnes (B.C.), the effort to reach hermitage,
sanctimonkio sweetbread, insatiable manougas, Guantanamo Weinerific,
"if you're going
to do it
with someone, I got dibs"—
embryo intruder Dr. Reese Yauch (L.P.), and his fizzay-sayon-see Nancy Diamond,
the effort to capitalize AIGHT, papal dependant Shife
and her private thought-jumper Ursula Shemp.

    "I stayed up thinking
    too much thinking I should
    think something I'm not
    wasting think on me wasting me
    on me"—Dr. Sleepy.

Lucinda and Kenry Lucaya, Dr. Pastis Valor and his reflection, this may tend
to go on but, it does end. Kona by the Sea, insta-Bardot memory stick,
Mrs. Leslie and Washington MOCA of the Contemporary Injection,
folding favor into fava beans and vespers, 1974's molten iris, your blank eye,

"the look"—of lava, gleaming corona of mankind
swallowed up by man spurt, in a single day
and night, twelve thousand years
in the rooting, for a spanking, Green Mercy Locursey and his Life Jacké,
Licky Rodando's wifey, a dandy echo shat,
to redirect some—here … is where you turn the book, pupils gone, convinced
all the girls look like her—the white-skinned blogger
the grand infidel practicing intimacy, Barbara Broccoli (B.C.).

"My husband Mary,
eat four Buffalini
be-fore-play"—say Hugh,
"it keps (sic) his cruelty,
down to earth."

Singapore guru Dr. Wei Siang Yu,
aphrodisiac completionist Frangelico (F.G.), synthetic concretist Frangelico (S.G.),
meditationist trumpetere amplifico Bradly Humpfard,
Ebay Pop Lock and his daughtette Wattup,
Mexico muscle relaxer, Ma Main Mamayan . . . El Incensivo del Fuego,
flustered Michelle (B.G.) flounders a truth in the tank,
"But, there's nothing, left, suk" (sic) mixed
with evaporation, desperation and damnation—Hugh, 35, hectic dogger
to husband Mary, 42, gropes the open window, lets Francis
simplify insertion, big O reminder, Jan and her mammarian debut, all of that now
seems sweet and lovely—
all that you used to avoid.

"Me
not eat
before come (sic)"—Eva Green, joyfully limitless, building a home
after Maitre D's and Latinos lounge in the hot tub, "Empee Freefro Licky!"
tricked out Fire Pig, Dr. Buddha Cap, Firefox Mandible, Dr. Cucoco, Dr. Cucotu.

Three months later, Hugh, 35, and yes . . . very very, is (sic sic) blinding the erratic,
"kiss kiss," Dr. Sleepy, bang bang specialist Shirley Bassé, Liverpool Plebian,
eco-friendly cataract Oddball Lamé, Dr. Crusader, 45, Laurentian Imitacio
and his waylord Dropstuff, 38, time remaining, not so fast, "and my tubes—

always ringing"—expecting
her husband Mary, every morning,
in April, "The I that knows everything,

is the I in it."

Swerver Says Sweeeee

let's say the weaver has a conversation with the thread
and the thread answers back with a tendril
let's say the tendril forms a rivering ribbon, cascading
from moon to weaver's tongue, let's say mouth misses
all the licks tongue used to play with, let's say licks
are silk, shining tufts of saliva fields, intertwirled
around each other
to form the one story that weaver has to say

and let's say
all this has light and morning, attached to its growl
and that twilight has no wash replacing light, no creation
beyond the interstitial grace of a single blue thread
flickering across the scar, of a slowly revolving lick

Three Spots under the Shade

~~~~a man

told me i was cerulean shear but only after a man
told me i was seeing eye but i dont want to be some gash you
are not grateful for your scars said a man
in cobalt sky spilled a crib singed for tie tot but i
dont want to be cerulean for you said he you are not for me
said crimson man to head half sheared half listening half bathing when
do you want your towel said i leave me when i exit said
skinny he mandarin all over sheared skin water lake
had double lake one under other and i thought imagine
that to have lake under lake for all days said
a man that i would walk in jasmine swim as breath
under head was juniper green rezoned for cerulean cumulo
combo rectus hand me said i my towel man gave me fan big as
thumbs i cant dry myself with this but you said he have
so much to show outside thumbs so much outside
fan wont ever swing but will cool dont said he hide i
stepped out of towel out of lake swung free by excess and
melancholy orange faded from limbs gathered to bone umber
cerulean melt on iris way down my ice cap do i said i
thank you now o man said he you are blue for indigo me
and nodding deep as ever bathtub reverie soaker be my eyes
again wont i said i be gash for a man sheared by magic
on a road of alabaster jubilee dripped from nose but i
dont want to be who only after i a gash a me
will ever tell who some azurean sea some sienna
scar be tot who tells said he a man who gashed his free
for thee

~~~~a bird

was cage below greybeard, was high above lady smelt by spin,
lets, do that agin she rhymed, anon provocateur martyrs doom
for mutual coma, right there, in our spin is . . . oooh how

easy to escape with winged hand and devil cape . . . if color
be speed, what start be light to white, says lady limbed
by taller spin, what afternoon does to cloud when legs
decide to never foot crotch, here, let's run digits
along limbic swimmers, take cored earthball, peel away
slept sheets, dripped in perspiring forevers, let's lay
remaining royalty side by side, marvel at the match of pore
with crik, curve the encounter between cliff and flesh,
negative outs seamed over positive ins, run
silver veins underneath crimson, creeping in cage, a
winged wake prepared for flight over silent skin, pecks at
life lived not loaned, mercurial bars blame bend for
bone, jewels robed in ravishing scars gash through
rivered hues of feet stuck in same blues, each drop dared
to float off diligent skin, this . . . evaporating cage, at once
sucked and milked . . . these interfered bars, left wet for
lick, man looks for lake, man . . . look at that lake

Skygrass

blackle-lutter-fly-tle-ly
kite-tle-lytle-hightle-I
browtle-owntle-lingle-wingle-lings
thingle-some'll-try

she is in black on white chair facing green mountain and white cow
I am in white on white chair facing her facing mountain
white butterflies white cow and brown bull a black
and white pattern in the green grass in front of her in front of me

seems like I could see the world
through her eyes I could see mountain and cow she sees
and past mountain over ocean she sees
and all pigment of natural sky and chemical skin
all canvas at foot beckoning step and line
all gesture past hand and fingernail she sees
all bone beyond wood
all full moon escapades
clear night's bluegreen attack on black
big dipper's steady wash over black and white seas
all see she sees

seems I could sway my tail to roman holidays
composed of floating violin plucks red orchestra plays crimson sky
neighborhood dog in brown invades my try seems
a shack catching sun on a mountainside rips the heart out of sky
showers out bluegrey chagalls flying white goats of horn
passing terra cotta sky seems if I try
I could see all she sees

but all I see
is black on white with green surrounding her
surrounding me

Infinity Song

when was it, 8 years ago
did we dare get lost
in what each would see
did I hear, that same music, stolen
from where we were, appearing
now, what, 8 years later
on the same exact coast
of some, far off visit
when we let, in this case, music,
or what follows after music, mostly
that slipped reminder, again, of age
or move, how everything smooth
was 8 years easier, but now
deeper, in a way quieter
to getting lost with someone
whose last name, is holding
your first

Bit by Bite

Fuzz or static
choose one, eight hours earlier and I
will ride your stream—the sleep you swim in
entire fields of feedback
prophesized as hair

Windswept across sierra plateaus
submerged by sandmen and water saints
Isadora's virgins—Goya's Saturn
carnivorous father hands me
clear strokes to behave

As if
drenched by howling dunes
across ancient bones—ambient feathers
on daughters, the size of fireworks
dormant little water bombs

Gathered by feral tomorrows
what's worse, a nation without a sun
or a moon—that's easy, no moon
without a sun
you only live in the dark

Which is blood
when slammed against
fly or mosquito—penetrate sublimity
through a mask of light
disguised as sweep

What is haze or fuzz to you
will someday ride the bare back
of your moonlit swims—a silhouette
of elegiac serenades, curved
along a color dreamed eight hours ago

Under Venus's Hair

I was told about the elephant and his million hands
By a mouse on the streets of Ave. A
In the falafel shop that sells veggie burgers
And vegan water a hole-in-the-wall with incense
And cranberry waffles I was told
Over a bowl of carrot-ginger soup that the mouse
Never sleeps afraid of being taken
By one of the elephant's million hands whose trunk
Was a dispatched stretch of road along America's highway
Whose wrinkled skin made mine much cleaner
Who changed shape in mid-sleep over an herbal tonic
And muffalatta stew on 7th Street & A
Where the 20-Something grit greets the morning rush
With an all-night fix the mouse without a voice told me
She was scared of sleeping and would I visit her dreamlife to help
Would I have room inside for an elephant's million wrinkles
Could I sweep away a corner in my dreamlife
To make room for a second of a highway's burnout over decaf
Soy cheese and hummus napkins could I give her mouse world
Another chance without talking she said this as I saw
In her one good eye a million reflections gently growing hands
On my way to work

A Story for America

Little Boy has nothing on
wants to have what Big Boy has
      wants to flex muscles he doesn't have yet
      wants to fly away from home
            looks back after taking two steps
            looks at his shadow
                  crawling up mountainside, up pyramids, up steps
                  back home

Little Boy sees the sun casting its light
& calls the sun: America
      America sees Little Boy screaming in playground
      & calls the boy: A Problem

Big Boy has left home already
doesn't see America as anything
      sees everything as sunshine
      sees into the sunshine
            gets blind from the sunshine
            & calls it: Tomorrow
                  Tomorrow sees Big Boy removes his eyesight
                  & calls him: Mine

Now Big Boy belongs to Tomorrow
has no one Today never Today
      Little Boy has Today before Tomorrow sees him, playing
      in Central, South, & other Americas
            Little Boy sees Tomorrow
            & calls Tomorrow: Mine

        little boy wants what big boy has
        big boy wants what little boy was
              they were two things marked the same thing
              & everyone is happening everywhere

they were two, by any chance
anybody see anything with nothing on it?
      by any hour, anyone see anything,
      by anywhere, see any place, we fill this room, with nothing, what?

      they were anything, anyplace
      they were nothing
      with anything on

Moroccan Highway

We have apologized for stepping on your beetle Marrakech, for swatting your tiny flies stuck to our walls impersonating cracks of plaster. We are Lions of destiny across an open desert, with hundreds of miles ahead of us, two lanes all the way. From the heat of Marrakech to the breeze of Essaouira, the Atlantic coast waits. One truck turns off, we wait to pass the next. Navigating highways on foreign soil is a mirage, of course *we're* foreign not the soil.

We've left the jesters of light and magic, the watersellers who will sell you the rain for a fair price. At the market, birthplace of hustlers and survivors, rival orange juice stands dot the border to compete for business—*20 cents a cup for fresh juice—19 cents my friend—18 cents my friend.* Snake charmers hypnotize cobras with sensory overload. Snake's skin is porous-reticulated-chain, lets every sound in—skin is sensory magnet for snake's body coiled on marketplace ground. They must feel-hear-see a million miles magnetized by light—if my every sense was heightened beyond recognition I'd be hypnotized into feats of superfluous fantasy too.

Pan-flutes and reed blowers penetrate steady rhythm of hand slappers. Arrythmitized mythics breathing ancient snores into smoked air. Swirled fabrics, vortexed heads, wrinkled facings, furrowed smiles—side by side with storytellers and griots. Multi-charactered one-man 'cyclopedias gifted with recollection, sharing a spot on history's time-patch, holding circles of listeners in tight attention who follow each movement with focused eyes. Birth of *Spoken Word* has no TV, word *is* TV. Watch as hands move eyes, string-taut-tight to fingers. To *rune* reality, to teller's *parablia*, to outcome of moral . . .

to window of burn, to smoked outdoor barbecue of dead baby lambs, to goat heads *complete* goat heads, to a feast of eyes and baby tongues, to ring bearers' come-ons, to whispers of pointed demons, to palms-up circumfery, to passers of light and dusk and outsider status, to maintaining different phases of full moon regalia—water savior on dry land, an oasis of profiles in a land of burnt skin. To the sellers of teeth on tables made of umbrellas, conical-headed priest against an outline of smoke, rising from infamous night stench.

Gutted mime bats a million lashes, circling a crowd of seers. Insider says to be outsider is to *be.* Yet Be'er says to be *inside* is. We pass fear of unknown on our Super Highway. Pass electric trees, shade that beckons. Desert is beauty to insular eyes of smoked city—better the smoke of sayers, smoke of magic outlined from night's carpet. Other taxis pass us, daring nonexistent speed laws. Existing the nonexistent resisting of sized existers. Reflection slays our distant vase, highway heat lines refract desert chops. Atlas Mountains by periphery—along road, women walk with balanced bundles on heads, postures and backs strong. Sense of straight is bred from ground up. Camels and donkeys grazing, acres of land around each, stone fence keeps the sheep in there is no gate, will keep the wolf out there is no wolf. Cows plod the road never stops.

We've crossed pinkies and have sworn to live *outcome* as it sways. To swim flow of life as each planned path is changed. As obstacles continue their insistence, as mounds appear in front, as each road absorbs the one ahead, as the open highway throws down its gauntlet. We cross pinkies as we travel the never-changing horizon, and swear to the journey ahead.

Rinse Cycle

Berber beach man buries his clothes
Under piles of sand
Near the surface he works carefully
15 minutes
Outlining wrinkles with sand
Then walks away

Berber man paces 20 paces
Counting each to start anew
7-year-old adventurer discovers & unearths treasure
Berber stands, paces back, gently
Educates boy to leave clothing alone
Boy leaves

Berber buries again
Then walks back to pile #2
This continues for one hour
15 minutes for each pile
4 piles at the compass points
One hour for the sun's heat to wash his clothing

Essaouira

Seaspray on pounded rocks
fiery windstorms crash
into hollowed shore
  the ocean waits outside this walled city
  Mogador glances
  from a distant island

at lowtide
you can walk to another kingdom
with the right shoes
  with the right twig
  you can paint an entire kingdom
  in one stroke

with the right stroke
you can say in one word
what a lifetime is waiting for
  and with the right life
  you can figure out—if the right life
  is the one you're in

When Does the Game Begin

Mogador is misted today, disappears into cerulean fog
Afternoon wind has died down
On the beach across Mogador
Little boys in skinny bathing suits roll in the sand
Taking advantage of rare calm
In a moment of non-windy sunshine, the beach is packed
With hundreds of boys the color of sand
In constant motion

Motion-creatures born for constant motion
Hand claps, polyrhythmic slaps, a hand game
For handsome chaps, little boys with Moroccan hair
Throw themselves into the sand

Over & over rolling around
They become the beach
An entire beach of sand boys
Hundreds of little bodies
For every particle of sand

Girls don't play with boys here
Barely any girls at all
At what age are they told to not play with boys
Are little boys told to stay away from them

Little girls should become a beach
One day for every particle of sand

Migration

Animals migrate in peripheral inversion—avoiding each other
without looking, arriving at their place
in a maturity of motion—an understanding of stoppage

In a yard of many humans
animals will gravitate towards similar patterns
what allows similarity—a similar human

The littlest one will appear through legs
through longer limbs the little ones swim—in a courtyard
of little boys, little girls will wait for a few years

Before smacking who allows to be smacked—sea gulls
will wait for the rise of tides and sleep, floating on what waves
allow themselves to be crashed—babies will run

As fast as they can, away from what allows them
freedom—in ancient courtyards freedom is as fast
as little boys can travel, in a field of sunflowers

The arc of the sun is where their faces follow—in a migration
of children, the ones who run outnumber
the ones who watch—seeing, being what animals

Grow into—children being
what adults grow into—boys being
as animal as boys

IV

Coney Island 1969

My father was the manager of Nathan's Hot Dogs on Coney Island
A memory inside a beach ball
My cousin reaching below the surface
Water in my lungs
Gagging
Blue sky
Technicolor white
Where skin should be

My father watched me walk the sidewalk cracks
From our bedroom window
In the Bronx
Asking me
What I thought I was doing
How a line is straight when you walk it
How a man knows exactly where to go

My father took us to Nathan's at Christmas
Company party
Santa
A thousand presents for each and every child
The boardwalk was cold
The rides empty
Coney Island winter
You had to warm your fingers
By hiding them from the ocean

My father gave us hot dogs and fries
Between his affairs
He gave me animals
To show his love
I had a beagle, a turtle, 3 guinea pigs and 2 java rice birds
I loved them
So I loved my father

My father took me and my two sisters to the Statue of Liberty
He told me it was made of Limburger Cheese
I loved him
He never hit me
He never hugged me
I had to walk straight
That's what he told me

When I visit my father
At St. Raymond's Cemetery
I find his gravestone
I have a son I tell him
Winter is our time
When he left
When all those presents at Nathan's were opened
All those families

My father towered over me
Laughing in his eyes
You're my little man he'd say
From up there
The bumper cars
The mirrors
All those reflections

My father had a relationship
With scale
An intuition for location
To remain
Long enough to be found
Calling to catch
What *will*
Does to *weight*

My father was never Coney Island to me
He never knocked on the door
That morning in the Bronx
My mother didn't open
No cops told her nothing

She didn't hide her face in her hands
No silent tears
No floor I play my indians on

No roller coaster tell me no turn
No question come from long legs
No mean kids
No skinny mirror
My father had yoga thumbs
Look what I can do I'd say
Leaning out just far enough
To make you catch me

Birthday Present; Birthday Boy

{these are the visual necessities} That which was
co-mingles—in sleep stupor; the following:
A white box, being carried by a perfect boy
in a white shirt—wishing; I were the boy
Or just the perfect; or maybe the shirt
inside the white box; giving me, the box of boy inside

Co; Mingling *{this is the vision}* the sleeves, to fit the box
so the boy—to fit the box, would fold my sleeves
To fit myself *inside* the shirt; so the boy
my classmate; a toy party; given—to me
The *perfect* boy in slowmotion *{the visual appears}*
the white box, glaring in the sun; I see him

Holding as it opens; to me *{I seem to reveal}* the white shirt inside
he is wearing; the white shirt box—inside, is a boy of me
Wearing what I am revealing; at my birth; my day; my toy party
my father *{this is what appears}* in my father's
Slow-motion giving of my party; standing over me—"Now,
what do you say, to the boy who gives you everything"

"Thank You"; he strides long strides—but not as long
as mine would become *{out of the picture}* he goes,
Thank you, or no; *{ force of habit}* already, there is only me
and the boy now; glowing *{out there—in this vision}* his perfect shirt
Catching sun; in slow-motion, the picture perfect white shirt
boy; as he glows to me—I take his hand, or hit him *{I am*

Unclear at this} but now; I am the window
looking down from three flights, before this all
Has happened; I am looking, still perfect—I see
the station wagon pull up; the boy comes out, wearing
A white shirt that glows; brighter than the sunshine
of my birthday party; the first to arrive

And in Trying

the boy tried writing about the sky
and in writing about the sky
he became the sky pretty gold and blue
and so he tried to write about the water
and in writing about the water
he became the water pretty gold and blue
and so he tried to write about the writing and in writing
the writing became pretty gold and blue
and so the boy tried leaving the writing
and in leaving he became pretty gold and blue
and so the boy became the water
and in watering the him his sky became
pretty gold and blue and so the blue tried
watering the sky and in writing about the boy
blue became pretty gold and boy and so
the gold tried writing about the pretty
and in pretty about the blue became boy boy and boy
and so the boy tried boying about the sky
and in skying the pretty pretty became
boy boy and boy and so boy boy and boy
and in boying the boy became
and gold and gold and gold tried golding the water
and in water was the blue who wrote about the boy
who tried writing about the sky

Terra Quad

what do you do
            when speed fracks cataclysm

            ...for you — terra non grata
            ...with molten being
            ...drilled into my dna — I waited
invisible prayer embedded
to invisible palm
            ...show yourself planet
            ...your layers
            ...stranded — in your After
with all us inbetweeners
inside
the bordered *Before*
            ...all you nowandthen'ers
            ...at the edge
            ...all the same — terra sin mecca
the salt in my beard
the bees throughout, all
the same

underneath
a roar — ten thousand times louder
than the one I stand on
spitting up dirty volcanos
in a direct fault-line
to who I am
            ...a century's blind telegram
            ...injects into your soil
            ...with every quake
there's only
so much
a planet can take
            ...only so much I thought I would have
            ...by now

>   *... is this, for anyone who needs it*
>   *... a day — grounded*
>   *... in prehistoric terrapins*

the mouth disappears
empty
the body the building the bone

orbit sage, omnipresent calliope
jesters in funeral gear
poets, poets, poets
>   *... easy to invent a word*
>   *... if language*
>   *... is what makes you*

>   *... if all I am*
>   *... is something to listen to*
>   *... something to step through*

slow down planet, your myth —
a smoke of contradictions
releasing debate
as healthy spillover — our only travel
an undercurrent of hidden language
that redefines *condition*
as *human*

telegraphic collisions — *terra cum voca*
of faith, of carnage
tremendous — your flow
>   *... and where to put that*
>   *... the answer — too private, paleontific*
>   *... angular*

somewhere in my daily commute
once I have nowhere to go — the birds and burns
that invigorate my step
will be the small crimes that stand out
once the big ones
have gone
>   *... waiting to be heard*
>   *... on the other side — this is not*
>   *... a scream for help*

... that happened already, a long time ago
... in the words — the work
... where scream happens
dressed in glyphics
secrets take on long tales
imagined — as language and line
... breaks — see, I'm not
... asking you about the asking
... just asking the teller for some quiet

... so I can hear
... the structure of my output
... and glance inside

... using you, dear planet
... as a guide, to just
... let go

**little orb. terror snort. spooner devil. tempter port.
thistle brush. invasion wing. leader wing.**

my boy, asleep on the living room couch
a tape recording of my voice telling him stories
my love, asleep on our bed
a recurring dream of us when we were flying
me, asleep in words
a poem's invasion of flight

why now — to feel active in *the walk*
to stir up the filtering capacity
of *the stranded*
to celebrate the work that does *the work*
the molecules, aligned for gulp

the air doesn't warn
anymore, just looks me in the eye
and says ... I'm here — are you?
... show me how your day
... moves you moves
... through you — takes so much

...to get through a day
...to put words into something, approaching
...thought
what you must be
going through, dear planet
your process
your disruption — aligned
with mine

what can I give you
when the ground won't stop
when a poem's invention
is both remedy
and opening

Waiting Young with Nothing There

newness saw its burst of numbness
tomorrow's nextness severs onceness

century's fabric flights across
a barely shouldered world

unformed midnight numbers many
hovers for a million soons

a street of wings where nows begin
in cloaks of unformed suns

       say this bigness plays with brightness
       rolling over urban onceness

       say this boldness stays with whatness
       calling out for swollen tearness

       sayness be my mouthness
       tongueness loveness lay such hardness

       sunless nightness try this muchness
       slay this fingrel's mighty yesness

severed city claiming swoon
I am one among your millions

flying suns among the brilliance
infant birthness barely tuned

I Saw You Empire State Building

I saw you Empire State Building
looking for your twin brothers
I saw you
watching your brothers burning
helpless to the ground
I look up at you, tall proud beacon
I too am a tower
it's my last name in Spanish

I look at you
glistening in the morning
shining at night I saw you
watching your brothers die
they were beautiful
and tall although
I think you have more character
but, older brothers wear their age well

I saw you helpless
and wanted to comfort you but
you're too big to hug
so I just keep looking at you
crying for you
holding you in my stare
us towers
we have to stick together

Me No Habla Spic

I remember one afternoon in soho
sitting on the sidewalk
with my long-haired cat harry
single and care-free
showing my beautiful pet to the world
people passing by, saying
what a cute spic

I remember my first day of my first job after college
running to catch the subway
wearing a maroon vest on a spring morning
passing under a pigeon's butt
dropping a wet one on my back, giving me
an aura I'd never live up to, people whispering on the platform,
what a cute spic

I remember my first poem
at an open mic, the host
announcing my name among the many
the crowd holding their applause
the bartender, the muse in the bathroom
the clergy at the front table, gathered in judgement
of a cute spic

I remember my first connection
between artifice and libido after my first show and tell
weaving that tendril of libertine inhalation
through the temporary airspace of second grade
my wet-spot palpable, little Veronica in polka dots
playing horsie with my hankie, thinking
what a cute spic

I remember the late night drink
set up by the
morning phone call on tenth street & avenue a

playing strip scrabble
on PCP, running out of letters
before socks, until the only words left were
what and cute

I remember my first assignment to compose a lecture
as a visiting professor, choosing as my topic
the apparent-only-to-me similarities between futurism's early fulcrum parades
and the first migration of nuyoricans, prompting the class
to pick through the paper's remains, leaving no grace or misguided flower child unlit
which subsequently sparked the chair of the department from her throne
to admonish, why bother with spic when the sixties have passed

I remember the city I love
reflected in plate glass
on a monday morning in midtown
jackhammers and blue skies
pierced though Chrysler, scraping miles
above the seething rush, breathless and barking
in unison, what a cute spic

I remember having the chance
to perform for the king
and my drummer using lipstick
to write a message on the king's giant ass
while I kept dancing, the audience
howling in underwear
that matched the failure of a cute spic

I remember a girl with my last name
who came up to me after a show
to tell me how
lots of people with my last name were watching me now
and that I needed to be responsible now
all the while me looking at her legs
thinking, what a cute spic

I remember my sisters
teaching me how to dance salsa
when I was in junior high
the hips following an island I'd never been on
politely holding my hand out
could I have this dance, my sister's knowing
tease, why yes you cute spic

I remember holding an umbrella for Debbie
in 7th grade after a dance
waiting for the bus, my first act
of chivalry before acne
the hot girl in class, under my umbrella
not looking or saying a word, on a rainy school night, but I'm sure
thinking, what a cute spic

I remember my uncle
taking me to cover a wedding, my main job
to hold the flash and eat free food
his humor continuing through the music that looked
and tasted like butter or was that cheese
on the car ride back, laughing non-stop at his own puerile stream
and me thinking, what a cute spic

I remember the audience levitating in the middle of a poem
just one mic on a slightly raised platform and me
shapeshifting through eyesight, the sound out of my pupils
blurred in an ocean of green effervescent inertia, the shapeless horde
hovering through the unbelievably intact embryonic fluid
of a star cluster's dna spiral, my spic-ness re-sourced
as kinetic quasars through light years of fragile diplomacy
thinking, it doesn't get any spic'er than this

I remember re-reading every email I sent
to feel as if I were the person
receiving my own words, basking in their clever reach
to feel the warmth of many messages
from many people, all of them me
a conglomerate of sinewy desperation
wrapped up in the viral opportunity of a cute spic

I remember carpet burns in the mail room
after months of talking a good game
finally having to prove to the well-equipped secretary
that of course I'd done it before, the cleaning lady
walking in on bone and flesh
pulled down to my ... oh is that, pardon ...
my cute, whoa

I remember the need to keep secrets
and hold onto what
no one else had, just to own something,
until my tummy hurt
and the stain that followed explained
a backlog of excess discolored by the lifelong
incineration of a cute spic

I remember performing a butoh dance
wearing nothing but a thong and black body paint,
an enigma hiding in full view
my older girlfriend's friend in the audience
confirming hydraulic suspension
both of them
nodding, cute and hmmm

I remember changing the lightbulb
for a smaller girl on the lower e
my long frame standing on a wooden crate
after a few bong hits, her hands
holding me steady by the hips
my belt lined-up with her brow, her lips
mouthing out, wota keyute spike

I remember skinny dipping
in an ocean after a reading and thinking
this feels great but first I need to get a reading
near an ocean for this to ever happen
as the naked yoga doppelganger compared tree
postures in the moonlight to my exposed id
while remaining balanced by the chant of speak with spic

I remember being trapped
by stanza and convention
where words had been withdrawn
from the vault of language I maintain
as an obelisk for rhizomic displays
of rendered territory flared into the stigma
of a tediously benign cute spic

I remember getting 50 cents
stolen from me by the bully
down the block, seeing an easy mark
in high-water pants with freshly bought Matchbox racer
held tight in my pocket, praying
he wouldn't force my hands out, laughing, as I walked off
to his bully friend, yo spic you think that's cute, punch

I remember being seduced
by the stage
wearing industrial foam on my head
while a ping pong ball
made its way from throat to hand
as my disembodied voice emerged through my rectum
offering the boatman's dilemma, how much for a cute spic

I remember running from a mouse
into the beehive
of a pajama party crosstown
slipping under the covers
before knowing what to do there
spooning in the wrong position while
fingering the button of a cute spic

I remember waking up one morning
from uneasy dreams and finding myself
transformed in my bed
into a giant cucaracha helpless on my back
draped under a flag of colors and shapes
I couldn't pronounce, my mom opening the shutters
letting the sun in, saying, oh what a beautiful spic

I remember the best of times
the worst of times, the age of wisdom
the age of foolishness, the epoch of disbelief, the season
of hope, the winter of despair, the morning of cocochi, having
everything before us, nothing direct to heaven
going the other way in short . . . the noisiest authority insisting
on the superlative degree comparable only to the tale of a cute spic

I remember the conceit of discovering
a catch-phrase built around identity
and how fleeting the prospect
of a fused mass, guided by skincolor before brainpower
the astral dimensions inherent
in a dna of parable presenting the overwhelming
differences that claim how the one is cute before the one is spic

I remember finding a banana peel
under a year's worth of newspapers, my refrigerator
duct-taped shut so I wouldn't be tempted to store even more
unopened containers and my sports jacket
ironed along a complication of creases to better present an
immaculately pressed emblem of normalcy
to the world outside my congested walls, what, a cute spic

I remember meeting the person I would spend my life with
and not knowing until years later
that I knew my life had just been completed
the first moment our eyes met
but not knowing that moment would not be realized
until many years after, lost in the time travel of love's engaged mess
by sonatas both cute and incomplete

I remember thinking I needed a format
to contain my writing and in the process
stumbling upon a giant machine that would one day
dictate to the world how to think and compose
sentences by stealing what had been written
and rearranging a sense of magnificence with a sense
of boredom into the, by now, stock regurgitations of a cute spic

I remember sitting in soho
with my two-year-old son
surrounded by expensive buildings
where there used to be none, the world passing
me, just thankful to get some rest
in the sun's imperfections, the people
ooh'ing and ahhh'ing... what a cute spic

Territory

The one time you were able
to have a decent conversation
with me, you sat direct in front.
I was on a sofa, you
on a table before me
slightly elevated. Looking
down you placed a hand
on my shoulder. Our friendship
a tangle of plateaus,
seer seeking sage.

At the crossroads, I've taken
to searching for the sturdiest
walking sticks. My dictionary
as reliable as it is
mercurial. A shifting table
of pulsing glossaries
whose index has yet to rust
but needs to be
watered, weeded
on every listen.

Which gate interprets,
which one rusts
and here
is where heart indulges mind.
Connection steady
as if definition
were faith
wondering which sits higher,
what friendship does
to time. To song, dear neighbor
how we always return.

Acknowledgments

The author wishes to thank the publishers and editors of the following books and journals for previous publication:

Bombay Gin: "Skygrass," "Moroccan Highway" (#30, 2004), "Terra Quad" (#38.2, 2012).

Brooklyn Rail (2012): "Apartment 5D," "The Circle at One End," "Waiting Young with Nothing There."

Chain (#7, 2000): "Birthday Present: Birthday Boy."

A Companion to Latina/o Studies, edited by Juan Flores and Renato Rosaldo (Malden, MA, and Oxford: Wiley-Blackwell, 2007): "I Wanted to Say Hello to the Salseros but My Hair Was a Mess."

Coon Bidness Magazine (2011): "Puerto Rican Astronaut."

A Gathering of the Tribes (#13, 2011): "Water."

Hanging Loose Magazine (#95, 2009): "Moth."

Heights of the Marvelous, edited by Todd Colby (NY: St. Martin's Griffin, 2000): "The Vase of the Universe."

Longshot Magazine (1998): "I Wanted to Say Hello to the Salseros but My Hair Was a Mess."

Lungfull Magazine (#20, 2012): "E.G. as I.E."

Me No Habla With Acento, edited by Emanuel Xavier (Hulls Cove, ME: Rebel Satori Press, 2011): "Father to Father," "Bit by Bite," "Me No Habla Spic."

1913 a journal of forms (#4, 2010): "Not So Fast Food," "Three Spots under the Shade."

Poems After the Attack, edited by Bob Holman and Margery Snyder (About.com Guides, 2001): "I Saw You Empire State Building."

Rhythm of Structure: Mathematics, Art and Poetic Reflection, catalog edited by John Sims (Sarasota, FL: Ringling College Selby Gallery, 2011): "Terra Quad."

Role Call, edited by Tony Medina, Samiya A. Bashir, and Quraysh Ali Lansana (Chicago: Third World Press, 2002): "A Story for America."

Vlag (#1, 2011): "Fixative."

Words In Your Face, edited by Cristin O'Keefe Aptowicz (NY: Soft Skull Press, 2007): "I Saw You Empire State Building."

XCP: Cross Cultural Poetics: "Song of the Red Lamb" (#7, 2000), "I Am Trying to Perfect My Assént (#20, 2008)."

About the Author

Edwin Torres is a poet and performer born in New York City. He is author of several poetry collections, including *Yes Thing, No Thing* (Roof Books, 2010), *In the Function of External Circumstances* (Nightboat Books, 2010), and *The PoPedology of an Ambient Language* (Atelos Books, 2008). His poetry appears in several notable anthologies, including *Post Modern American Poetry* (Norton, 2013), *The Best American Poetry, 2004* (Scribner, 2005), and *ALOUD: Voices from The Nuyorican Poets Café* (Holt, 1994). He has been a visiting writer and instructor to workshops and writing programs across America, and his CD *Holy Kid* (Kill Rock Stars, 1998) was included in the Whitney Museum's exhibit *The American Century Pt. II*. He has received fellowships from the Foundation for Contemporary Performance Art, the New York Foundation for the Arts, and the Lower Manhattan Cultural Council, among others, and is featured on poetry websites, including the Poetry Foundation and Poetry Society of America.